# The Spur Book
## of
# Trout Fishing

# The Spur Book
## of
# Trout Fishing

MICHAEL BRANDER

SPURBOOKS

Published by
SPURBOOKS
(a division of Holmes McDougall Ltd)
Allander House
137-141 Leith Walk
EDINBURGH EH6 8NS

ISBN 0 7157 2063 5

© Michael Brander 1981

For
Angus and Andrew

# CONTENTS

# PREFACE

I was fortunate in being taken in hand by a keen fishing uncle at a tender age, and I started fishing at the age of eight with my own rod. Watching my uncle, I learned unconsciously a lot about the ways of trout, in the river and the loch, and also about handling a rod, casting and hooking, playing and netting a fish. With the introduction of fresh materials and fresh ideas over the years I have frequently had to relearn my fishing methods and it sometimes surprises me, in view of so many modern innovations, that fish were ever caught in years past. There may not have been the same pressures on fishing waters, and trout may not have been as sophisticated as they are today under a constant barrage of artificial flies and lures, but fish were caught then in considerable numbers and the thrill remains exactly the same today.

The brown trout, or *Salmo trutta*, is amongst the most sporting, adaptable and wariest of game fish and has the virtue of being present almost everywhere in the United Kingdom, as well as in many other parts of the world. In addition the rainbow trout, or *Salmo irideus*, has been widely introduced into British waters and can also supply the angler with good sport. In so far as it is possible I hope this short introduction will point beginners in the right direction and start them on many years of enjoyment with rod and line. Like me, they will soon discover that there is a great deal to learn and just when they feel they have mastered one aspect of the trout's behaviour they may find they have to revise their opinions again. That is one of the lasting pleasures of trout fishing, but the thrill of catching, playing and netting a fish always remains the same.

# Chapter 1

# WHERE TO START

## Journals

It is all very well deciding to start trout fishing, but if you are a complete beginner the problem is to know where to turn for advice in the first place. Failing any knowledgeable friends or relations, the only answer is to look for some other source of help and information. One obvious method is to start by buying one or more of such publications as *The Angling Times, Trout and Salmon, Trout Fisherman,* or others of a similar nature. Even if some of the articles or technical terms used are at first incomprehensible, there should be sufficient evocative material to whet the appetite, but, more to the point, there will also be advertisements offering tuition in all aspects of trout fishing.

Such advertisments may offer anything from individual tuition at a fishing school or centre, to holiday courses of a week or more on a well known river, loch or reservoir, based on a local hotel and run by a well known fisherman. Some hotels also offer tuition in various aspects of fishing, from casting, playing and netting a fish to fly-tying under expert guidance. It must also be pointed out that in some areas there are evening classes available, on subjects ranging from trout fishing to fly-tying, arranged by local authorities.

## Tackle Shops

In addition, any reputable fishing tackle shop is generally a ready source of help and advice. Indeed, the beginner without any other sources of information would almost certainly find that as good a plan as any would be to go along to such a shop and explain the situation. This is not such a rash idea as it might appear at first sight, since any worthwhile fishing tackle retailer knows that if he provides the beginner with friendly advice and sells him a rod, reel and other tackle suitable for his needs, as well as advising him where to go to obtain tuition and catch trout, he will almost certainly have a satisfied customer on his hands who will return to him again and again. His biggest problem is likely to lie in preventing the novice from buying extra tackle which he is never likely to require. Once in a tackle shop there are many otherwise level-headed anglers who are unable to prevent themselves buying equipment which is totally unnecessary, but which happens to catch their fancy.

**Licences and Permits**

At this stage the point must be made that there is an important and basic difference between fishing for trout in Scotland and in England. In Scotland trout fishing is free to everyone. In England a rod licence is required from the Regional Water Authority before anyone may fish. Such licences vary in cost from region to region, as do the wording of the regulations governing fishing, and the opening and closing dates of the season, which may vary considerably from March to October. It is important to have such a licence and carry it with you when fishing, since the water bailiffs are entitled to confiscate fishing tackle and institute proceedings against those fishing without one.

In addition to the rod licence for the region, local permits are almost always required in both England and Scotland from the fishery controlling the water on which you intend to fish. These may be day permits or season tickets; they are obtainable in some instances from the Regional Water Authority, where it controls the fishings, or through the bailiffs, or from agents such as local fishing hotels, or fishing tackle shops. The method of obtaining permits to fish individual waters varies from water to water, but lists of waters offering a day's fishing are from time to time published in the fishing journals mentioned above. Once again, the advertisments in these journals are worth reading for this purpose.

**Clubs**

Finally, another method of both obtaining fishing and, very probably, tuition is to join a trout fishing club. Most towns of any size near good fishing waters have such a local club and they are usually keen to have new members. Here again the reputable fishing tackle retailer is likely to provide the name of the secretary and advice on membership. Very often such clubs have their own waters which their members are entitled to fish free, or at nominal cost.

# Chapter 2

## FISHING TACKLE

It has already been intimated that the average fishing tackle shop has sufficient aids to fishing to lure even the experienced angler from his senses. There is indeed an amazing choice of tackle, sufficient, it would seem, to ensure that everyone catches fish even in the most adverse circumstances. At first sight there would appear to be a rod for every purpose and reels, lines, flies and lures in even greater profusion, leaving aside such questions as nets, fishing bags and other ancillaries. To some extent, of course, your tackle may vary according to the type of trout fishing you are most likely to encounter, whether in large or small rivers, lochs or reservoirs, but to begin with it really is not necessary to acquire too much equipment until you know how to use the basics and can assess for yourself what your further requirements are likely to be. Thus, since by far the largest proportion of fishing waters are restricted to fly fishing only, it is sensible to start with a view to fly fishing. For this initially you will need:

**Rod**
Different rods will have different degrees of bend in them and this is known as the rod 'action'. There are stiffish rods, where the action is restricted to the tip, and rods with more action from the middle to the tip. There are also rods which bend from the butt right through to the tip, known as a butt action. Such a rod with a slow butt action makes for longer casting, but the beginner may find a rod with a stiffer action easier to handle at first.

It has been argued that the ideal fly-casting rod should be built in one piece, since theoretically this would provide the perfect action. Such rods can be obtained, despite their obvious drawback as regards carriage from place to place. In practice most fly rods are made in two, three, or even more jointed sections, generally carried in a canvas rod case for convenience.

A typical three-piece fly rod would consist of a butt section with a cork handle and alloy, or metal, screw fitting to hold the reel securely in position at the base. The short length of rod on

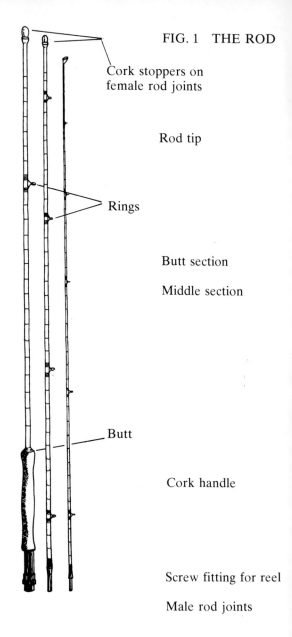

FIG. 1  THE ROD

Cork stoppers on
female rod joints

Rod tip

Rings

Butt section

Middle section

Butt

Cork handle

Screw fitting for reel

Male rod joints

14

this butt section projecting beyond the cork handle will usually have a porcelain-lined intermediate ring to carry the line from the reel without chafing. The middle section, which fits into the butt section by a male suction joint, or ferrule, as it is termed, sometimes with an additional screw clip, will generally have two or more intermediate rings to carry the line. The rod tip section which fits into the middle section by means of another male suction joint, or ferrule, generally has further intermediate rings and a porcelain-lined top ring to prevent the line chafing when casting or playing a fish. When the rod is mounted in once piece the rings of each section should be exactly opposite each other to allow the line free passage from reel to rod tip and thus obtain the best results from the rod's action.

The rod may be made from various materials, although greenheart rods, like hickory shafted golf clubs, are no longer commonly made. Carbon fibre, or graphite, rods are the latest and still amongst the most expensive available, being extremely light and powerful as well as easy to handle. They enable the experienced angler to make long casts with the minimum of effort, but it may be argued that some makes leave a little to be desired when playing a powerful fish, and should they receive a blow when under stress they may be liable to break. On the whole they are not really to be recommended for the beginner until he knows what he wants from a rod and can assess his own requirements for himself.

One of the old stand-bys is the split-cane rod, which is made from cane split into six sections and then glued together. A split-cane rod is pleasant to handle, gives hard wear, and can be had in a variety of actions. It is also likely to be quite expensive, and again is possibly not the ideal rod for the beginner.

Perhaps the commonest rod-making material today is fibre-glass, which is tough and light, and is usually used to make a rod of hollow construction. Carbon fibre rods with fibre-glass centres are now on the market, and some such combination may well prove the basis for rods in the future. With both fibre-glass and carbon fibre, or graphite, it is possible to buy outfits ready for assembly to build your own rod. On the whole, my suggestion would be that the beginner should start by buying himself a fibre-glass rod of about 8 feet

6 inches in length. Whether you buy one ready-made, or prefer to make up your own, is largely up to you. Such a rod will probably be quite sufficient to serve as an all-purpose fly rod for most fishing conditions you are likely to encounter initially.

**Reels**

There are numerous varieties of reel to choose from, but they do not need to be expensive. The important points to ensure are (a) that it can hold sufficient line for your purpose and (b) that its weight suits the rod you have bought. It is desirable, therefore, to try the reel with the rod to ensure that it is not too heavy and does not interfere with the balance. It is advisable to buy a reel with interchangeable spools, since this means that should you wish to do so you can change the weight, or type, of line you are using with the minimum of trouble. Alternatively, you may prefer to have two reels with the same end in mind. A second reel in any event is a sound investment, since it is always possible for one to jam, or break, in the middle of a day's fishing, which can be irritating to say the least.

**Lines**

*Weight.* The line has a great deal to do with the ability of the angler to cast well and should, like the reel, be suited to the rod. Most rods manufactured nowadays have the approved line weight, which is regarded by the maker as most suited to it, stamped on the butt. Using a line too light for the rod will make for difficulty in casting, especially into the wind, while using a line which is too heavy for it is likely to damage the rod itself.

*Buoyancy.* It is possible to obtain lines of many kinds, but mostly today they are made of a plastic coating over a tough Terylene plaited inner core. It is possible to buy lines with a greater or lesser degree of air incorporated in minute bubbles in the plastic, designed to keep the line afloat. The degree of buoyancy can be varied so that the entire line remains floating, or so that the tip of the line sinks, or so that the entire line sinks slowly, or alternatively quickly. The latter lines have lead incorporated in the core to provide a line which instantly sinks deeply. Whether you require a line which floats or sinks depends, of course, on the type of fishing you are attempting. Usually it is desirable to have one line which floats well and another which sinks, at least partially; hence the desirability of having interchangeable spools, or else two reels. My own choice is for a floating line for almost all forms of fly fishing, but there are occasions when an alternative is desirable.

*Taper.* In addition to floating or sinking lines it is possible to buy lines of varying thickness. For instance, there is a double taper line which has a gentle taper towards each end and is thickest in the middle. This allows for more delicate presentation of the nylon cast, or leader, to which the fly is attached. Furthermore, as one end wears out, the line may be reversed on the reel and used afresh from the other end, thus giving it a double life. Although this type of line does not allow for lengthy casting, it is probably the best to use when beginning. A forward taper line, thicker at the end than in the middle, also known as a weight forward line, has been developed to allow for longer casting, if at the expense of delicacy of presentation. The double taper line is usually preferred on rivers, while the forward taper, or weight forward line, is more commonly used on reservoirs where lengthy casting is often considered desirable. A further refinement of the weight forward line is the shooting head, which is merely some ten yards of line attached to a nylon backing on the reel. The heavier weight of the line when cast shoots the lighter nylon with it and allows for very lengthy casts, but this is not a method recommended for beginners.

*Backing.* Anything from ten to twenty-five yards of Terylene line may be wound onto the reel drum first as a 'backing' for the proper line. The two lines should be spliced together to allow the join to slide easily through the rod rings. This allows scope for the angler when there is a possibility of catching large trout. More backing is likely to be required in open spaces such as lochs and reservoirs than in rivers, but the amount of backing used must necessarily be limited by the size of the reel.

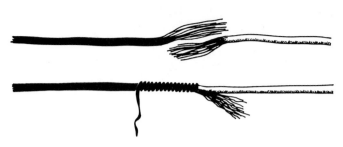

FIG. 2   SPLICING

**Cast, or Leader**

Attached to the line it is necessary to have a nylon cast, or leader, some ten or more feet long, to which the fly or flies are tied. A cast may be bought ready made from the tackle shop. It may be a tapered cast, which is more expensive, or it may be of one width throughout. It may have one or more 'droppers', or short lengths of nylon about three inches long, attached to it at intervals of some three feet from the end to which flies are attached. For the purposes of wet fly fishing one or two such droppers are recommended, providing a tail fly on the end, a dropper, and a 'bob' fly. The 'bob' fly bobs along the surface of the water as the cast is drawn in. Although it is possible to buy

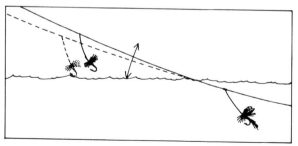

FIG. 3   THE ACTION OF THE BOB FLY ON THE WATER

such casts ready made, it is simple enough to make up your own, either tapered with graduated breaking strains of nylon, or with one length of nylon with droppers at suitable intervals. For the beginner it is good practice to make your own casts, or leaders, since the tying of knots joining two pieces of nylon is something at which every angler has to become proficient, and the sooner he starts the better.

## Flies and Fly Boxes

Artificial flies come in numerous sizes and almost every shape and colour. Suggestions as to the most suitable choices will come later. The fly box in which they are kept is, however, part of the fishing equipment to be considered here. There are various kinds: those with clips, foam, felt or magnets to hold the flies, and others with compartments for the flies and Perspex tops through which the flies are visible. I prefer the last, since the flies can be seen at a glance without opening the box. Of the others I prefer the magnetic kind, since there is a danger of clips damaging the barbs or hooks or of the hooks becoming rusty in wet foam or felt. It is, however, largely a matter for individual preference. Some form of fly box is undoubtedly required, and it is not desirable to have them all jumbled together.

## Net

There are numbers of collapsible and telescopic patent nets to be had and in general they are quite useful devices. It is also possible to buy plain round nets, which screw into a wooden, or alloy, handle. These provide a useful wading staff, should one be required, and there is no danger of them collapsing or not telescoping due to having got some dirt in their mechanism. I have used both kinds and will continue to do so, but I always tend to feel more comfortable with a plain round net, even if it may be a little more trouble to set up and take down.

## Fishing Bag

All sorts and sizes of fishing bags are available and it is again largely up to the individual what size and kind he buys. An adjustable strap, so that the bag can be slung over the shoulder and fits comfortably, is essential. I like one with some spare pockets in which to stow the spare paraphernalia that inevitably accumulates, such as a spare reel, fly box, a spring balance to weigh the catch, a small handy priest, or weighted cosh, to despatch the fish, and so on. A useful tip with any bag consistently used for fishing is to carry in it several plastic bin liners. These can be used for carrying any fish caught, and save the trouble of cleaning out the inside of the bag, which even if it has a removable plastic lining will tend to get smelly in course of time.

### Waders
Chest waders are not really necessary for trout fishing, but a pair of good thigh waders are virtually essential. They are easy enough to walk in and even where no wading is intended they are good protection against brambles and similar hazards. Thigh waders with studded soles are the best kind; they should be stored hanging upside down in a dry cupboard when not in use.

### Clothing and Other Tackle
Waterproof clothing is absolutely essential. A sound plan is to wear a showerproof jacket and carry a lightweight windproof and waterproof over-jacket rolled up in the fishing bag. It is also desirable to have a lightweight pair of nylon waterproof overtrousers, which too can be readily carried in the fishing bag. In the pockets of the jacket it is useful to have:

A pair of Polaroid spectacles, which cut out glare from the water and can help you to see trout on occasions much more clearly.

A sharp knife, useful for gutting trout, and preferably one with a pair of scissors and a disgorger for removing hooks from a fish's throat. Special anglers' knives with these attachments are available and are useful. The scissors for cutting nylon can save considerable tooth wear.

Line and line floatants ready to apply to line or fly to keep them afloat are also best kept at hand in a convenient pocket. Special anglers' waistcoats, worn over the top of other clothes, are often advertised, and the principle behind them is that they dispense with a fishing bag and have a place for everything. I have never tried one, but it is only fair to admit that I have friends who swear by them. It is equally fair to say they are not necessary for a beginner. A good peaked waterproof hat or cap is certainly an asset. The 'twa-snouter' (Sherlock Holmes's headgear) has many advantages in keeping the sun out of the eyes and the rain off the back of the neck. It can also be worn with flaps down to keep the ears warm when required.

# Chapter 3

# THE TROUT AND ITS ENVIRONMENT

## Water acidity

The degree of alkaline or acid content of any water to a large extent determines the size of the trout in it. A high alkaline content, such as is found in chalk and limestone areas, promotes a plentiful insect life, as well as crustacea such as shrimps and crayfish. In waters with a greater acid content, such as are to be found in peaty, or moorland, areas, insect life is not as abundant, nor are there likely to be many other forms of feeding. It follows naturally that fish in alkaline waters have a higher growth rate then those in acid waters.

## Rate of Flow

Another feature affecting growth rate is the flow rate of the water. In general, the faster a river flows, the lower the growth rate of the fish, since less is available to eat. Small crustacea and plant life are unlikely to be able to establish themselves where the rate of flow is too fast. In general trout will always inhabit those areas in any water where they can obtain the most food with the least expenditure of effort. In any fast-flowing water they will be found in the shelter of rocks, or in areas of slack water, or similar comparatively sheltered places. Compared with the trout living in slower-flowing waters where food is readily available, the ones in faster-flowing waters clearly have a more difficult struggle to survive and it is not surprising that they do not generally grow to anything like the same size.

## Types of Fishing Waters

On the whole the majority of fishing waters can be classified in five broad categories. There are the major rivers such as the Tweed, the Tay, the Avon, the Wye and many others of a similar nature, which are rain fed from numerous feeder streams. These can be as much as fifty or more yards across and may be fished from boats, by wading, or from the bank. They are subject to floods, when the water is muddy and unfishable. There are also large lochs, lakes and reservoirs;

these last provide a very high proportion of the fishing available in England. These may also be fished by boat, or from the bank, or from the edge of the water, and are often stocked with brown and rainbow trout.

There are smaller lochs, or lakes, or man-made ponds, such as gravel pits, which are frequently highly stocked and form a special fishery. These can provide good sport on the put-and-take principle (i.e. regularly re-stocking to make up for fish caught), much depending on the surroundings. These again may sometimes be fished from a boat, but more generally from the water's edge. There are also smaller streams, or burns, which may provide excellent sport in varied surroundings fished either from the bank, stalking individual trout, or by wading, often little more than ankle, or knee, deep. In the West Country, in Wales, and in Scotland such fishing is quite common.

Finally there are the chalk streams, found mostly in Hampshire, Wiltshire, Dorset and Berkshire, apart from a few in Kent, Derbyshire and Yorkshire. These are generally heavily preserved and plentifully stocked. They can provide challenging and also, in certain circumstances, surprisingly easy fishing. Mostly situated in lush southern pastureland, they are well worth investigation. The dry-fly and up-stream nymph are the main methods of fishing the chalk streams and the individual fish has to be marked and stalked, which is pleasantly satisfying, but the same can be true of other forms of fishing.

It is untrue, however, to say that the trout from each of these environments is exactly the same fish. Indeed a trout taken from one end of a loch, or reservoir, where it has been feeding on a muddy bottom, may be dark and eel-like, whereas another feeding at the other end on a different diet may be sleek, full-bellied and golden coloured with a fine showing of spots on its sides. Their flesh may be equally different, the one white and the other pink coloured.

The hand-reared, freshly released rainbow, which has been fed on special pellets all its life, may seem a fine fish when he is hooked and will no doubt play well enough, even if he is an innocent to the slaughter when it comes to detecting the difference between a poorly cast fly and the real thing. He is a very different fish from the wild brown trout which has lived all its life in the harsh world of the river or loch. Such a fish is generally wary and harder to catch and even if smaller the victory is very much greater.

There are, however, various points these fish have in common, whether hand-reared innocent or wary old trout of many seasons' experience. Their field of vision in either case is restricted to an area of water above their head. It should also be remembered that by and large the trout will be looking up-stream, since that is the general direction from which its food is likely to appear. While their vision may be restricted it is still not desirable to stand silhouetted in full view on the bank of a river or other water. Nor, since a trout is very sensitive to vibrations, is it advisable to stump around the bank or splash around the water. Move carefully in or near the water.

## Chapter 4

## FLIES, NYMPHS AND LURES

**Types of Artificial Flies**

Artificial flies and nymphs are generally intended to be imitations of natural insects attractive to trout. The aim is usually to copy as closely as possible those insects on which the trout are feeding and place the artificial imitation as naturally as possible near to a fish in the hope that it will mistake this for the real thing. This may be done by floating the artificial imitation on the surface of the water, as with the dry fly, or by sinking it beneath the surface, as with the wet fly, or with the nymph.

Dry flies are usually tied with a hackle, or long thin feather, wound round the hook to resemble the wings, thorax and legs of the natural fly, at the same time aiding buoyancy. These flies are tied with a cock bird's hackle which, being firmer than a hen's, tends to float better and dry flies are mostly used in clear, comparatively slow-flowing, or calm water, particularly where trout may be seen feeding. The aim is to float the dry fly naturally over the circles left on the surface by the feeding trout.

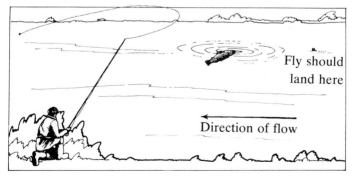

Fly should land here

Direction of flow

FIG. 4    STALKING A RISING TROUT WITH DRY FLY

The wet flies and the nymphs are generally tied with hen bird's hackles which, being softer, are more inclined to sink. The wet flies are mostly used where there is a ripple on the water or in fast-flowing water, and are allowed to float naturally with the current. The nymphs may be used in conditions suitable for either dry or wet flies where trout are seen feeding beneath the surface, causing a bulge on the water as they arch their backs. With both wet flies and nymphs it is sometimes worth twitching, or working, them slightly at intervals in the water to give the impression of a struggling insect.

Those wet flies which are brightly tinselled and resemble no known fly may more properly be termed lures and are generally worked across fast flowing, or rippling, water, in a series of jerks, thus perhaps exciting the trout's curiosity, or resembling some small fish. The same method is generally used with proper lures, which are intended to imitate small fish such as minnows, or worms, or crustacea such as fresh-water shrimps. The number of brightly coloured wet flies and lures which are obtainable in any fishing tackle shop is quite remarkable and the beginner would be wise at the start to concentrate on imitating as far as possible the natural insects on which the trout seem to be feeding.

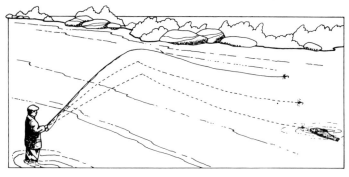

FIG. 5   WET FLY FISHING (DOWNSTREAM)

**Natural Flies**

Throughout the year there are certain times of the day when insects of one sort or another tend to be particularly attractive to trout. There is what is known as the 'Duffer's fortnight' on the chalk streams of the south, when Mayfly are hatching; the trout go mad, leaping after every hatching Mayfly they see. There are times, such as these, when anyone casting, no matter how clumsily, will still catch fish. There are also times, on any water, when flies of some sort are hatching and the 'rise' is on. The trick then is to imitate as closely as possible the natural fly on which the trout are feeding, but this is often easier said than done.

There are few things more maddening than having trout rising all around you and being unable to match the natural fly. In such cases, however much you may cast over rising fish, they simply ignore your fly in their haste to take the natural ones on which they are feeding. Once the rise is over, conversely, you may catch a trout on your previously scorned artificial. Such is the way of fishing. There is usually some comparatively simple solution, but it is not always easy to find it.

It is important to understand the life cycle of the aquatic fly. The eggs are laid under water on stones, gravel, or similar places by the female spinners. The eggs develop into nymphs. The maturing nymph develops wing cases and surfaces to hatch as a dun. (See Fig. 8 for the difference between this and sedge.) The duns then moult and turn into spinners. The spinners mate and the male spinner dies, while the female spinner lays her eggs under water, thus perpetuating the life cycle, before dying in her turn. At various stages of its life the aquatic fly provides a desirable source of food for trout, and each stage can be imitated successfully.

Perhaps the commonest group of flies to be found hatching on the water during the fishing season are the duns, much copied in artificials. Amongst the most common of the duns is the Large Dark Olive, which is usually to be found in the early part of the season, in April/May and again later in September/October, particularly on rivers. Rather smaller and a little paler is the Medium Olive, mostly found from May to September, but commonest of all is the Blue Winged Olive, which may be found all through the season, particularly from the end of June.

# FIG. 6   THE AQUATIC FLY'S LIFE CYCLE

b   Nymphs with rudimentary wing cases hatch from the eggs

a   Female Spinners lay their eggs in water

c   As the Nymphs mature their wing cases develop fully

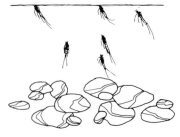

d   The Nymphs rise to the surface to hatch

e   The Duns hatch from the Nymphs and take flight

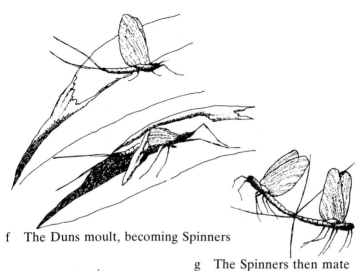

f   The Duns moult, becoming Spinners

g   The Spinners then mate

h   The Spinner
    females lay their
    eggs by (i) drop-
    ping clusters or by
    (ii) releasing groups
    of twos or threes
    or (iii) underwater

(i)

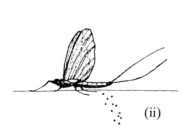

(ii)

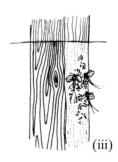

(iii)

Others of interest to the angler are the Mayfly, which is well known in the south and is likely to hatch in the afternoons from the last week in May to the second week in June. Although the Mayfly is less common in Scotland, an artificial version is still likely to prove effective on occasions. The March Brown is another well known large fly, generally hatching in April, and mostly found in rivers, particularly in fast water. The hatches do not usually last long.

Another important group of aquatic flies are the sedges, of which there are numerous variations, both in size and colour, but mostly tending to be favoured in the evening. Stoneflies, which may be as large as half an inch to an inch in length, are also often a useful lure when worked across fast moving water. There are also smuts, which hatch out from the reeds and are often a source of food for trout as they hatch during mid-summer. Finally there are the chironimids, or midges, all too prevalent, on many waters, for the angler to overlook them. The midge pupae, which lie in the water film before the chironimid emerges, can be readily imitated and are well worth trying when the trout are feeding on them.

In addition, of course, there are various crustacea, shrimps and snails, as well as a few land insects appearing fortuitously on the water, which are included in the trout's diet. The latter may sometimes be instantly snapped up by trout as if they were exactly what they had been waiting for, while they continue to disregard every other enticement. Thus caterpillars, worms, spiders, gnats, moths and other creatures may prove well worth imitating. The nub of the matter, once again, is to find what the trout are feeding on.

**Selecting the Right Fly**
This is where time spent on observation can save a lot of time wasted on fruitless fishing, and can result in catching fish where others fail. Of course, if a glance at the fishing record book indicates that certain flies are currently proving successful, this may save a lot of trouble. Then again, a helpful water bailiff, or other source of local wisdom, may also provide useful advice; but such aids to fishing are not always available, nor always reliable. The best source of information undoubtedly is the first trout caught. By examining the

stomach contents with the aid of a sharp knife, or if you prefer it with one of those stomach pumps, consisting of a plastic tube and bulb, available from most tackle shops, you should see at once on what the trout are feeding. It is then a question of matching the fly, nymph, or other stomach contents, as closely as possible. Thereafter, in theory, all should be easy. That this is not always so is one of the attractions of fishing, but these preparations certainly provide a head start.

When the fly, or nymph, has been duly matched and still the trout refuse to be interested, the solution ought to be that there is something wrong with the presentation. It may be that the size of the fly is wrong, or the hook too prominent. It may be that the wet fly should be worked more vigorously across the current, or more slowly. The dry fly should perhaps be presented on a finer length of nylon, or that nymph fished deeper, or nearer the surface, or more slowly.

**Hooks**

When the trout are showing interest but apparently 'taking short' or rising to the fly but not being hooked, the solution very often lies in the hook itself. It is always worth inspecting the flies, or lures, after each fish has been caught, or if a stick or stone has been caught, even for an instant. It is very easy for a barb to be snapped off and there is nothing more annoying than losing the chance of a fish through some elementary carelessness such as this, even if it is common enough.

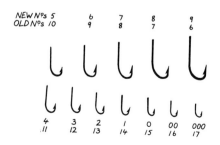

FIG. 7 · HOOK SIZES

# FIG. 8   NATURAL FLIES AND LURES

a   Sedge

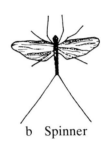

b   Spinner

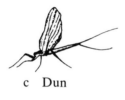

c   Dun

d   Shrimp

e   Sedge Pupa

f   Olive Dun

# FIG. 9   ARTIFICIAL FLIES AND LURES

a   Artificial Sedge

b   Artificial Spinner

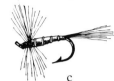

c   Artificial Dun

d   Artificial Shrimp

f   Greenwell's Glory
(representing Olive Dun)

e   Artificial Sedge Pupa

h   Artificial Midge Pupa

g   Artificial Nymph

The size of hook used must vary according to the circumstances. For loch fishing in Scotland the size may vary from No. 12 to No. 16, dependent on matching whatever is being taken. For evening fishing and the further south one goes, conversely, smaller hook sizes are probably required. The old saying 'the brighter the sky the brighter the fly' is still not without justification, and the converse 'the darker the sky the darker the fly' is also true within reason.

**Wet Flies**

A wet fly fisherman's cast, likely to be effective in many conditions, might consist of a March Brown on the tail, reminiscent of a blue winged olive dun, a Greenwell's Glory on the dropper, reminiscent of a dark olive dun, and a Silver Butcher on the bob, likely to attract the attention of the curious trout. An Invicta on the bob, reminiscent of a hatching sedge, and a White Chomper on the dropper, reminiscent of a small pupa, might also prove successful. There are countless variations, but the aim should be to attempt to imitate food on which the trout are known to be feeding, or alternatively to have been feeding, since the latter is sometimes as effective.

Other popular and effective wet flies commonly used on many lochs and rivers in varying sizes are: Alexandra: Coachman: Dunkeld: Mallard and Claret: Peter Ross: Teal and Silver: Spider (various patterns): Wickham's Fancy: Zulu.

Useful underwater flies, nymphs and lures, which are likely to catch trout in the right circumstances, are:

Corixa (or Water Boatmen): Chompers (designed by Richard Walker): Grey Goose Nymph: Hatching Sedge: PVC Nymph: Pheasant Tail Nymph: Midge Pupa: Shrimp.

**Dry Flies**

The standard dry flies used in most waters in various sizes to suit the circumstances are:

*The Duns.* Blue Dun: Gold Ribbed Hare's Ear: Greenwell's Glory: Grey Duster: Iron Blue: Mayfly: March Brown: Orange Quill: Tup's Indispensable.

*Others.* Black Gnat: Caperer: Coch-y-Bonddhu: Pheasant Tail Spinner: Red Sedge.

Amongst the more common lures it might be as well to mention the well-known worm fly and the fly minnow. There are many more, and every tackle shop will have something special which is ideal locally.

## Making Your Own Flies

It is well worth the beginner starting by learning to make his own flies. It is surprisingly simple and outfits complete with all the necessary materials, including a small vice to hold the hook, are readily obtainable from most tackle shops. Once the basic principles have been understood it does not take long to make up a fly to a chosen pattern and there is considerable satisfaction in catching a trout on a fly, nymph or lure you have made, especially if you have matched a natural insect.

In most cases the beginner who has started to make his own flies will very readily be able to make his own according to a similar pattern. With the aid of one or two books suggested in the bibliography he will find making his own artificial flies, nymphs or lures is well worth while in that he learns a great deal more about the trout as a result. This in turn should lead to catching more, and to greater enjoyment.

# Chapter 5

## PREPARATION AND PRACTICE

### Before you Set Out

The first stage is to ensure that all the required tackle is to hand, including the all important rod licence and fishing permit. Thereafter it is merely a question of arriving at the water at a suitable time to ensure that the morning rise is not missed and that every opportunity is available to catch fish. The rod itself may be transported in a fitting on the roof of a car, with the butt foremost as it should always be carried, or it may be in the rod case ready to be put together on arrival. The reel, with backing already spliced to the line, with spare spool, or reel, to hand should be ready for the day's fishing. The cast, with flies already selected and tied in place, may be ready for tying to the end of the line, or at least a cast, or leader is ready to tie to the line prior to a decision on the flies most suitable after investigating the situation. All the rest of the tackle, net, flies, nylon and so on should be in the fishing bag or on your person, but always check carefully before leaving, for it is certain that if anything is left behind that is the day when it will be most required. Sod's Law operates with absolute inevitability in such cases.

### Getting Ready

On arrival at the water it is then a question of assembling the rod, attaching the reel to the butt, leading out the line correctly through the rings of the rod (not missing any out in the process), then joining the end of the line to the cast with a simple Figure-of-Eight knot. At this stage it is as well to have mastered the few knots which are required when fishing. These are:

*The Full Blood knot,* as shown in Fig. 10a, used to join two pieces of nylon and, if necessary, provide a dropper for a fly in a wet fly cast.

*The Turle knot,* as shown in Fig. 10b, to hold a fly firmly in place on the end of the cast, or dropper.

*The Figure-of-Eight knot,* as shown in Fig. 11, to join the cast to the line.

## FIG. 10A THE FULL BLOOD KNOT FOR JOINING LENGTHS OF NYLON

i

ii

## FIG. 10B THE TURLE KNOT FOR TYING FLY TO CAST

## FIG. 11 THE FIGURE OF EIGHT KNOT FOR JOINING LINE TO CAST

FIG. 12  THE NEEDLE KNOT FOR ATTACHING
        LEADER

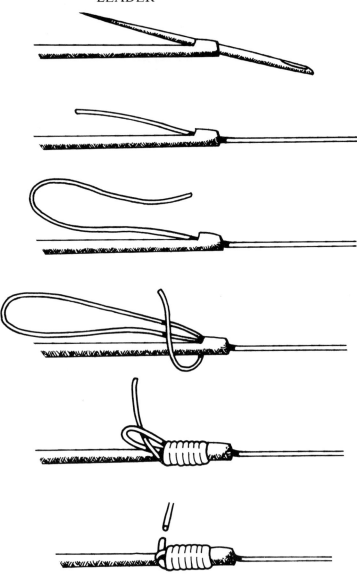

38

*The Needle knot,* as shown in Fig. 12, for joining a tapered leader to the line, so that the join does not stick in the rod rings, allowing for longer casting.

If dry fly fishing, or nymphing, the appropriate fly, or nymph, will be attached to the cast by means of a Turle knot. The cast itself will probably be about the same length as the rod, nine feet, or thereabouts. If wet fly fishing the droppers will be at about yard intervals from the tail fly. Thus the bob fly will be some six feet from the tail fly and about a further three feet from the line itself. The dropper will be about three inches long and the aim will be to drift the bob along the surface of the water, while the other two flies are sunk, one just below the surface film, and the tail fly about six inches down.

## Casting

Armed with rod, tackle, net, licence, spare flies and the rest of his gear the angler is now ready to take to the water. Whether this is a question of fishing from a boat or wading, the mechanics of casting remain much the same. The emphasis should be on allowing the rod to do most of the work. In order to make a simple straightforward cast a certain amount of line, say three or four yards, should be stripped off the reel with the left hand initially. The rod should then be drawn back to approximately twelve o'clock, with the elbow tucked into the lower ribs and the wrist unbending. The thumb should be pointing up the butt and as the rod is raised vertically the line in the left hand should be released. When the thumb and butt are nearly vertical, almost level with the eyes, the line should be all released and it will be found to be straight out from the rod tip behind the shoulder. At this point the reverse action should start taking place and the rod should start moving forward to the ten o'clock position again. The tip of the rod will bend and perform the regular miracle known as casting the line.

It is advisable to start by practising on dry land, aiming at some object laid on the ground, such as the lid of a shoebox. The secret is to pause very briefly in the twelve o'clock position before moving the arm and rod forward again. It is also important never to make any jerky movements of the arm, or bend the wrist, thus producing a whip-lash effect which often causes the fly, or flies, to be cracked off the line. After a little practice co-ordination will be achieved and casting will

# FIG. 13   THREE-FLY CAST

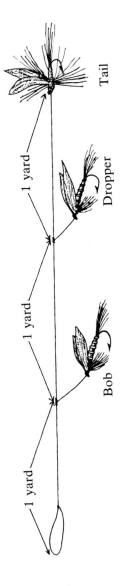

become a simple and automatic matter, while a considerable degree of accuracy can soon be obtained. In due course, also, the beginner will be able to release more line while casting, known as shooting the line, to gain distance. Backhand casting, rather similar to a back hand tennis or squash shot, will also soon be mastered, enabling the angler to cast comfortably in the stern part of a boat, or to avoid trees or bushes on the shore, when a forehand cast might become entangled. More advanced casting can be left for the future. This is sufficient to enable the beginner to catch fish successfully.

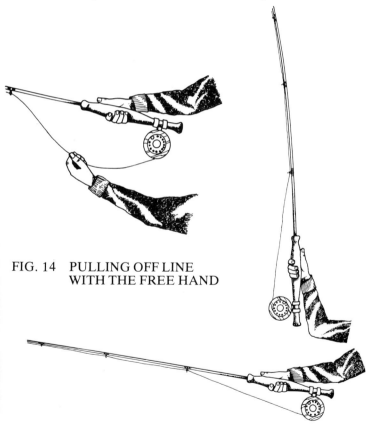

FIG. 14   PULLING OFF LINE
WITH THE FREE HAND

FIG. 15   THE CORRECT WAY TO HOLD THE ROD

# FIG. 16  CASTING

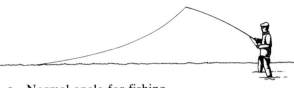

a  Normal angle for fishing

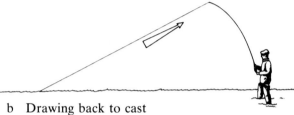

b  Drawing back to cast

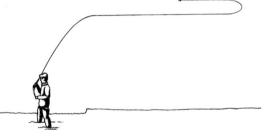

c  Pause at shoulder height to allow line to straighten

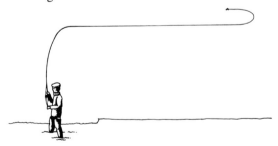

d  Start of forward cast

## Covering the Water

The angler can take advantage of the trout's comparatively limited field of vision by casting upstream, so that the fly appears as naturally as possible above the fish. It is thus possible to 'cover the water', by gradually casting in an ever increasing circumference. Initially the angler's casts will cover an area comparatively close at hand; then gradually the length of the casts will be increased so that the area covered is enlarged systematically. Finally the angler will be covering all the water within range. At this stage he or she will move on a few paces, thus steadily and systematically covering all the water available and allowing the fly, or flies, to appear in the most natural manner possible over the whole area within casting range. Each trout there, whether lying behind a suitable rock, or cruising around, will have an opportunity to inspect the fly and decide whether to take it or reject it. If, after such systematic presentation, the fly proves of no interest, it should be changed for another closer to any natural fly on which the trout appear to be feeding.

## Mending the Line

When casting a fly, or flies, in a comparatively fast flowing water it is sometimes difficult to prevent a line from being carried ahead of the flies in a deep semi-circle, eventually causing the flies to skitter across the surface, or drag, in a most unnatural manner. This 'bellying' of the line can result in fish being lost, or alarmed, unnecessarily. The solution to this bellying problem is to drop the rod point just before the line gets out of control and then raise it again with a semi-circular motion towards the run of the current. This will cause the line, hopefully, to perform a neat parabola, as with a skipping rope, and settle in a semi-circle facing the other way, thus allowing the fly, or flies, to continue to float naturally. This simple action is known technically as 'mending' the line. Although easily enough mastered, this can be a very important technique when fishing across a river into the slower shallows on the far side.

Whether casting with dry fly, nymph, lure, or wet flies the angler should have one aim in mind apart from such systematic presentation as outlined above. That aim should be to main-

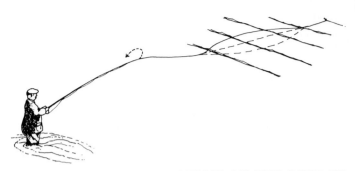

FIG. 17   MENDING THE BELLY ON THE LINE TO
PREVENT DRAG

tain a line as nearly straight as possible between the slightly
raised point of the rod tip and the line as the cast is gradually
retrieved, or followed. All the angler's concentration should
be on the point where the line, or cast, can be seen to enter the
water. As that moves, so the rod tip should follow, maintaining
constant contact with it. In certain cases, as when fishing a
nymph just beneath the surface, the rod point may be twitched
occasionally to simulate movement. Similarly, wet flies in fast
water may be worked by vigorous movement of the rod point
and by pulling the line with the left hand, but concentration
throughout should be on the point where the line, or cast,
enters the water.

**Striking**
Sometimes a take will be signalled by a splash, or boil, apparently some distance from the fly, but in general the first sign of
a trout taking the fly, or lure, is a movement of the line or cast
at the point where it enters the water. As soon as that line
moves, no matter how slightly, no matter what way, whether
sideways, downwards, or forwards, be it only as much as a
quiver, or hesitation, the rod point should be raised. This is
known as 'striking' the fish. The object is to hook the barb
deeply into the trout's jaw, preferably into the corner, as it
feels the fly. This instant reaction to the fish taking the fly is the
secret of catching trout. If the trout is allowed sufficient time
to take the fly into its mouth and realise that is it not the juicy
morsel it imagined, it will promptly spit it out, and that will be

another trout lost. It is usually better to strike at an imagined rise rather than wait too long when in doubt.

It is important, on the other hand, never to strike too hard at a taking fish. The rod point should merely be raised, although on occasions it may be sound practice to pull on the line with the left hand at the same time, if there is a lot of line out. The rod point should never be jerked backwards so that the fish is not only hooked but sometimes, in the case of a small trout, hauled bodily out of the water. In the case of a large trout in similar circumstances the line would simply be broken immediately and the fly and part of the cast left in its jaws. It must be borne in mind that very often the breaking strain of the nylon next to the fly is not much more than three pounds and this may have been weakened with wear and tear. If a trout is struck too heavily in these circumstances it is only too easy to lose it and the fly.

**Playing the Trout**
Similarly, once the trout has been hooked, it is advisable not to put too much pressure on it if you have a cast with a light breaking strain. This can call for finesse and discretion when playing a trout, to prevent it reaching the safety of a reed bed, or winding the cast round a boulder, root, or other obstacle. If the trout can achieve such objectives he is very likely to have broken the cast and won the day. By using the rod to the maximum and trying to steer him away from such hazards, the angler can counter the trout's sudden dashes. The angler may occasionally recover line onto the reel when the trout moves towards the bank, or boat, but mostly should counter the fish's struggles by keeping the rod point up all the time and allowing the bend of the rod to tire the fish.

Maintaining pressure through the rod is the first essential. The only time the rod point must be lowered is when the trout comes to the surface and leaps. Then the tip of the rod must instantly be lowered to slacken the tension on the line or the trout may fall back on it at full tension and break it. As soon as the trout submerges again the constant pressure of the rod must be maintained by raising the rod point once more.

## Landing the Catch

The stage will finally come when the trout's struggles begin to weaken. At last he may be seen to turn sideways on and then the battle is nearly over. It is advisable, however to get the net well into the water before leading the beaten fish over it, for the sight of it may often cause him to make a last dash with sometimes unfortunate results. Once fairly in the net swing the trout firmly into the boat or onto the bank, for many fish have been lost even at this last moment when, with the pressure off, the hook gave way.

If it is then desired to return the trout to the water unharmed for any reason (for instance if it is undersized) it is desirable to try to detach the hook with the minimum amount of handling. It is best if possible to keep the trout in the net, shake the hook free, if feasible, and then return the fish to the water. The more the trout is handled the less are its chances of survival on being returned to the water.

To kill the trout a sharp blow with a heavy blunt instrument (e.g. a 'priest') behind the head will have the desired effect. It is highly undesirable to leave a trout kicking in the bottom of the boat, or on the bank. Quite apart from the humanitarian aspect it is not impossible for them to leap into the water again.

## Cooking Trout

With a large trout of one to two pounds or more the best method of cooking to my mind is baking. Prepare the trout by gutting and cleaning, removing the head and tail if so desired, then dry it and cut shallow slantwise slits, just breaking the skin, about an inch apart down both sides. Sprinkle with salt and pepper on both sides then brush liberally with melted butter and put into an oven about 350° to 400°F until cooked. Serve with a cucumber or meunière sauce.

For a small trout of under a pound the best method of cooking is undoubtedly in oatmeal. After gutting and cleaning, dry it and brush with a beaten egg. Then dip it in fine or medium oatmeal and crisp fry it in deep fat, for about eight minutes. Serve with a large slice of lemon as garnish. There is no better way of eating trout for breakfast, or indeed, of that size, at any time.

Chapter 6

## PLACES AND METHODS

### Large Lochs, Lakes, or Reservoirs

Faced at first with a vast expanse of water it is often difficult to know where to begin. There are, however, certain cast-iron rules. Trout will go where the best feeding is available. In any large expanse of water the prevailing wind undoubtedly drives food towards one shore or another. If you are bank fishing then that is where you should go; do not be surprised if the trout are feeding not only well within casting range but almost against the edge. The wind may be against you but there is nothing to stop you casting at an angle to the bank, covering your water steadily as you move forward. If you decide to wade, make sure that you cover all the water you intend to wade before entering it and alarming any trout in the vicinity. Try not to present a silhouette on the bank against the water. Remember that any promontory, bay, or stream leading into the water — even a jetty sticking out — will have its resident trout patrolling the area, and it is largely a matter of ensuring that you provide a suitable fly, or lure, in the right place.

When fishing wet fly from the bank or from a boat it is desirable to have a very slight ripple on the water. In a boat there are certain rules to observe. It is essential to choose a 'drift' whereby the boat floats slowly downwind in the direction desired. Setting the boat sideways on to the wind is quite a simple matter, after a little practice in controlling the boat with one oar and fishing with the other hand. The drift should normally be fairly close to the shore, aiming at covering the area where the shallows slope into the depths, indicated usually by a darker line. The idea should be to drift so that one rod can fish up to the shoreline and the other cover the area over the deeper water. The bob fly should be allowed just to dangle in the ripple and the line should be steadily drawn back as the boat drifts.

Any islands, or promontories, or mouths of streams or burns entering the larger water should be carefully fished, since there are certain to be resident fish in that area. Any indications of shallow water, such as reeds, or wind currents on

47

the water, may be regarded as likely to be productive. It is always advantageous if a map of the water is available, since knowledge of the deeper and shallower areas can save a great deal of guesswork in strange territory.

In reservoirs in England there may be considerable shallow water before any depth is reached, and this may mean wading out some way before reaching the fishable water favoured by trout, where the deeper water begins. The tendency in these circumstances is to feel that the further one can cast, the larger the fish is likely to be. It may, however, often be found on careful observation of the lie of the land that such long casting is not required. Indeed, some of the best places for trout in reservoirs or any large water are often surprisingly close to shore.

When there is a dead calm on the water, whether fishing from boat or from the bank, the dry fly, nymph and similar lures come into their own. It is an object lesson then to learn how many trout there are in the waters that previously seemed empty of fish. Accurate casting to individual feeding fish is then the most effective method, but first it is essential to discover on what they are feeding.

*Dapping.* This is one other method of fishing the larger loch, or reservoir, which has not been mentioned. This is best practised from a boat, although it can be done while wading, or from the bank at a pinch. A longish rod is required, generally about fourteen feet long, and a large dapping fly. A Mayfly is frequently used, but a Great Gnat (or Daddy-Longlegs) or large Sedge will work well. A floss line is used to attach the fly to the line, since the object of the exercise is to allow the fly to float out on the wind and dance on the waves in front of the angler. The ideal conditions are therefore with a goodish wind raising a sizeable wave and probably a sunny day in May or June, or even later in the season. The floss catches the wind and the fly dances on the water and some surprisingly large trout may be caught in these unlikely conditions.

## Larger Rivers

These are another instance where it is frequently unnecessary to make longer casts. Careful study of the water and steady fishing of the likely spots on your side of the bank are often far more likely to produce results than ever longer casting to try to reach the greener pastures close to the further bank. Upstream wet fly fishing, or nymphing, can be very effective on such a large river, but careful coverage of the water is essential. Downstream wet fly fishing, working the fly in the rougher patches, or runs, can also prove very effective. Advantage should always be taken of any patches of shade when the sun is shining brightly, and fishing from light to shade can be effective on occasions.

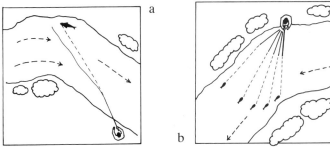

FIG. 18   a   FISHING THE DRY FLY (UPSTREAM)
           b   FISHING THE WET FLY (DOWNSTREAM)

In the larger river there are invariably patches where the undergrowth on the bank provides an overhang, frequently over a deepish pool of water. Places such as this are well worth working over with an artificial imitation of some land–borne insect such as a caterpillar or a spider. Such a lure, dropped quite splashily on the surface of the water, can lead to a memorable trout being caught.

Alternatively, there are times when the dry fly is the only answer, but on a river of any size there is always likely to be the problem of line belly, resulting in constant line mending to avoid drag. Despite this there are certain to be reasonable runs and slow patches where the dry fly can be effective. In certain circumstances it is even feasible and effective to try a little dapping, especially in the summer months when conditions are suitable.

## Smaller Lakes or Lochs

The smaller lake, or loch, can often provide excellent sport. In the south the smaller lake, working on the put-and-take principle, can be a source of very good sport. There is usually a limit on the size, of course, as well as the bag, and such sport is not likely to be cheap, but it can be instructive. Either the dry or wet fly, or the nymph, may be used depending on the conditions and circumstances. Boats are not usually common, but there are exceptions.

In Scotland, Wales and Ireland the smaller hill loch may often provide quite surprisingly good sport. Although the trout may be small there are likely to be some good fish, and since they are generally not greatly fished they are often very unsophisticated and readily take any fly or lure. This can often prove exciting fishing, providing a worthwhile bag.


## Small Streams or Burns

Fishing the small stream, or burn, can be great fun as well as exciting sport. Mostly this is dry fly fishing, although upstream worming, akin to upstream nymphing with a worm in place of the nymph, and every bit as difficult, may be tried. Here the individual trout may be seen and stalked, keeping under cover of bush, or bank, sometimes kneeling on hands and knees, sometimes forcing one's way under overhanging bushes, casting lines with surprising sideways casts to set a fly above a monster trout of a pound, or even a pound and a half. The average keepable fish may be little more than half a pound, although many smaller may be caught, but what excellent sport they can provide! The chance of scientific casting, or mending line, if there is any belly on it, is remote in these microscopic versions of the larger river. The West Country, Devon and Dartmoor, North Wales (especially around Snowdon), and Scotland from the Borders north, provide hill burns and small streams of this kind where great sport can be had. The bag may not appear much, although extremely good eating, but the sport to be had from such a day's trouting, with a seven-foot rod and a light line, can be memorable indeed.

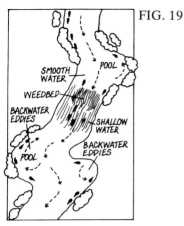 FIG. 19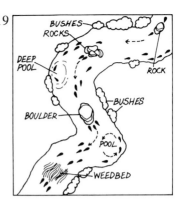

a  TYPICAL LOWLAND
   STREAM

b  TYPICAL HIGHLAND
   BURN

**Chalk Stream Fishing**

The chalk stream fishing is mainly dry fly, or else upstream nymphing. Here the fish are likely to be well fed and scattered fairly evenly through the water. Reed beds, fences, inlet streams, or drains, bridges and weirs are all likely to hold fish in such water. With any rise visible it is a question of stalking the rising fish and laying the fly over him in as natural a manner as possible. Then, with good fortune, the fly will be swallowed and the fight is on. Although this is amongst the most expensive fishing in the United Kingdom, it has reasonable claim to provide value for money. It costs £50 a day (1981 prices), but is probably worth it to those who can afford it.

**Put-and-Take Fishing**

Privately stocked waters where rainbow trout of vast size are to be caught are now quite common in the United Kingdom. Not so long ago I was a guest on a private stretch of not much more than three quarters of a mile of a backwater of the Avon in Hampshire. Although not much more than twenty feet across, it was stocked with rainbow trout of eight pounds or more. By upstream nymphing and entirely fair fishing I caught forty-six pound weight or thereabouts of rainbow and brown trout within an hour and a half. I say 'thereabouts', since most

51

of those fish went back unharmed and unweighed, simply because I had no desire to damage my host's stocks. Yet, although it may seem to some the height of ingratitude, I think I would sooner have caught one three-pounder on a large river or even just a small bag of half-pounders on a hill burn, given the same fishing time over again. Fishing should never become too easy. It is only fair to add that the same host subsequently took me to fish the wonderfully named River Piddle in Dorset, where I caught my permitted limit of two two-pound rainbows and greatly enjoyed myself, and was defeated by a large brown trout on the same day. That was a much more memorable occasion, to my mind!

Chapter 7

## ADDITIONAL POINTS

### Litter
The essence of fishing is enjoyment, and it ill behoves any angler to spoil the enjoyment of others. This can be done very easily in many ways. For instance, it can be easily done simply by leaving litter around. In particular, no angler should leave lengths of nylon about, with which wretched wild birds invariably become entangled. Any other form of litter is simply bad manners. Especially is this the case regarding boats which have been left badly anchored, full of beer cans, or odds and ends of sandwiches and so on. Gates, it should scarcely need to be emphasised, should be shut behind one and this also applies to the doors of boathouses and similar places into which sheep, or children, may blunder with dire results. Have a thought for your fellow angler and other users of the countryside at all times.

### Courtesy
Courtesy when fishing is also something that should not need emphasis, yet by my observation it clearly does. When fishing in a boat it is highly undesirable to crowd any other boat, or, if using an outboard motor, to pass close to another boat fishing on a drift. It is, of course, bad manners to cut in front of another boat where the occupants are clearly drifting downwind in your general direction. If you wish to take the same line, then come in some distance behind them. Oddly enough this can often prove very effective tactics since after their passing the fish may be in a taking mood.

Even where a permit allows spinning, it is the height of bad manners to spin within range of someone who is fly fishing. Nor in any circumstances should one fly fisherman crowd another on a river or loch. If any angler happens to be on the water first in any area (and there may be considerable competition for the privilege) he has the right to be there and it is up to the others to move in behind him. In a reservoir, when still-water angling, this may not apply in quite the same way, since not infrequently it is necessary to fish within quite close proximity of another angler, but approximately forty yards distance should be kept, even then, wherever possible. In no circumstances should one angler fish across another.

When fishing from a boat with two rods it is also absolutely essential that each angler stays entirely within his own area and does not cross the other's line. It is the height of rudeness, as well as crass stupidity, to cast at a rising fish across the other angler in a boat. Lines may be crossed all too easily in a boat, inevitably with dire results, without actually courting trouble.

When fishing from a boat it is also desirable never to crowd any angler fishing from the bank. Similarly, those wading should always have a care since they may well frighten fish over a large area. For the same reason it is common sense as well as courteous behaviour not to walk along a bank where other people are fishing. The thumping of heavy feet is quite enough to spoil their fishing. It should hardly need to be added that transistor radios played loudly are just as offensive to the fish as to fellow anglers. If you have to carry one then have the courtesy to use earphones. You might even catch some fish then!

# FURTHER READING

*The Pursuit of Stillwater Trout:* Brian Clark (A. & C. Black/ Pan)
*Trout Fly Recognition:* John Goddard (A. & C. Black)
*Nymph Fishing in Practice:* Oliver Kite (Barrie & Jenkins)
*Nymphs and the Trout:* Frank Sawyer (A. & C. Black)
*The Flydresser's Guide:* J. Veniard (A. & C. Black)
*Fishing for Lake Trout:* Conrad Voss Bark (H. F. Witherby)

# GLOSSARY OF TERMS

**Amadou:** An absorbent fungus used to dry the fly when it loses buoyancy through becoming wet when dry fly fishing.

**Artificial Fly:** An imitation of a fly, another insect, larva or small fish, manufactured from feathers, fur, silk, thread, tinsel or similar materials around a hook to attract fish.

**Backing:** A cheaper line used on a fishing reel below the principal line but spliced to it to provide a safe margin should a large fish take out a great deal of line.

**Belly:** Of a line, to float in a curve between the rod point and the fly, or flies, causing them to react unnaturally.

**Blood Knot:** A knot used to join different lengths of nylon securely (see Fig. 10A).

**Bob:** The description used for the top dropper on a wet fly cast, because it bobs on the surface of the water. Hence bob fly.

**Bulging Rise:** The bulge on the surface caused by a fish feeding on flies or nymphs beneath the surface of the water.

**Cast (or Leader):** The length of tapered nylon between the line on the reel and the artificial fly.

**Chironimids:** Midges.

**Close Season:** The period when fishing is not allowed, which may vary from March to October with considerable local variations.

**Dap:** To fish by letting the fly bounce gently on the surface of the water.

**Double taper line:** A line with a taper at each end providing double life.

**Drag:** The movement of the artificial fly on the water when the current is affecting the line.

**Drift:** The line which one chooses to cover when drifting a boat down a loch in front of the wind; on this depends much of the success of the fishing.

**Dropper:** The fly, or flies, attached to a wet fly cast by a 3-inch length of nylon.

**Dry Fly:** An artificial fly designed to float on the surface.

**Dun:** A fly which has emerged from the nymphal stage prior to making its first flight.

**Ephemeridae:** A class of fly of great interest and importance to the angler. See life cycle of aquatic fly: p. 28.

**Ferrule:** The joint, of metal or plastic or similar material, used to join the various sections of a fishing rod. Male or female suction joints.

**Fly Box:** A box specially designed for holding flies.

**Fly Rod:** A rod especially designed for fly fishing.

**Hook:** The bent and barbed piece of steel on which the fly is tied. The scale of measurement used for trout hooks is generally known as the New scale (see Fig. 7).

**Landing Net:** Net used for landing fish.

**Leader (or Cast):** See Cast.

**Mending the Line:** Raising the rod tip and by a quick movement reversing the belly of the line caused by current to reverse the drag on the line.

**Nylon:** A synthetic material used by anglers for casts and for spinning lines.

**Nymph:** The larval stage of aquatic insects.

**Playing a fish:** Maintaining the maximum strain consistent with the strength of the tackle.

**Priest:** A weighted club for killing fish when landed.

**Rod:** The balanced length of wood, or other material to which the reel and line are attached and with which the angler casts his fly and plays the fish.

**Rod rings:** The rings attached to the rod through which the line runs.

**Strike:** The action of raising the rod point or of tightening the line to drive the hook into the trout's jaw.

**Tackle:** All apparatus connected with fishing.

**Trout (brown):** A freshwater game fish commonly found throughout the U.K.

**Trout (rainbow):** A freshwater game fish introduced to this country from California and now frequently used to stock water.

**Turle knot:** A knot used for attaching fly to cast (see Fig. 10B).

**Worm fly:** A dark Palmer fly mounted in tandem with two bodies and two hooks, but only one eye, mostly used under trees, or bushes, where trout may be feeding on caterpillars.

# the great
# OUTDOORS

The walking, camping and
backpacking magazine
recommended by
the Rambler's Association

Holmes McDougall Publications

# Climber

## & rambler

**Britain's leading outdoor adventure magazine and the journal of the British Mountaineering Council**

Holmes McDougall Publications